BREAKING  FREE

FROM

STRESS

HOUSE

LINDA MINTLE, PH.D.

BREAKING FREE FROM STRESS
by Linda S. Mintle, Ph.D.
Published by Charisma House
A part of Strang Communications Company
600 Rinehart Road
Lake Mary, Florida 32746
www.charismahouse.com

Unless otherwise noted, all Scripture quotations are from the Holy Bible, New International Version. Copyright © 1973, 1978, 1984, International Bible Society. Used by permission.

Scripture quotations marked AMP are from the Amplified Bible. Old Testament copyright © 1965, 1987 by the Zondervan Corporation. The Amplified New Testament copyright © 1954, 1958, 1987 by the Lockman Foundation. Used by permission.

Scripture quotations marked NKJV are from the New King James Version of the Bible. Copyright © 1979, 1980, 1982 by Thomas Nelson, Inc., publishers. Used by permission.

Cover design by Debbie Lewis
Interior design by David Bilby

Library of Congress Catalog Card Number: 2002108795

International Standard Book Number: 0-88419-896-0

This book is not therapy or counseling, nor does it provide clinical advice and treatment. Readers are advised to consult their physicians or professional mental health providers when dealing with mental health and medical issues. Neither the publisher nor the author takes any responsibility for any possible consequences from any treatment, action or application of information in this book to any particular reader. In regard to stories, names, places and all identifying details have been changed and altered to protect the privacy and anonymity of individuals who may share any similarities or shared experiences. People references are actually composites of a number of people who share similar issues and are equally protected with names and information changes to remain confidential. Any similarity between the names and stories of individuals described in this book and individuals known to readers is purely coincidental and not intentional.

02 03 04 05 06 — 8 7 6 5 4 3 2 1
Printed in the United States of America

Without stress, there would be no life.

—HANS SELYE

CONTENTS

"I can't handle one m o r e thing in my day!"

"I really need a break!"

"The kids are driving me crazy!"

"What if I lose my job?"

"I don't want to face the day."

"I feel like I'm going **CRAZY**."

"WILL I EVER HAVE DOWN TIME?"

"I just want to scream!"

"I'm putting in too many l o n g n i g h t s."

"It's all **overwhelming!**"

"Will this rat race ever stop?"

"Help! I'm stressed out!!"

Stress is all around us—a couple breaks up, your marriage is in trouble, illness hits, your company downsizes, a parent dies, classes are too hard, terrorism abounds. At times life feels overwhelming.

Stress is a by-product of our postmodern living. We have too little time, too few resources and little control over most things in our lives. Stress can be generated by an event such as divorce, death, illness, watching the news or the tragedy of 9/11. Some stressful events, like the birth of a baby, are predictable. Others, as in the case of disaster, are not.

Stressful events can be ongoing or resolved quickly. They can be related to life transitions, the environment, development or our perceptions of things. They may be avoided or unavoidable, mild or severe.

Stress can also be a *response* to events. Things happen, and we become fearful, anxious and depressed. We carry stress in our bodies and in our minds, and we worry about the lack of control we feel over certain things. Stress, if not managed properly, disrupts our sense of well-being and can lead to the development of anxiety disorders and physical symptoms.

Because stress is inevitable, you need to know what to do when it hits. Your ability to cope is related, in part, to the resources you have. Resources can be things like money, education, intelligence, power, self-confidence and other internal and external qualities. But as a Christian, the most important resource you possess is your standing with Christ. Here's why.

In times of stress, remember you have an unlimited resource in God.

Resources can be depleted over time. When stress is chronic and seems unending, your resources are taxed. For example, maybe you started out with enough money to handle unemployment, but over time the money runs out. Or maybe you were very confident raising children, but that last child wore you down. Resources are usually limited. But God is an unlimited resource that can be accessed continuously. His promises never run out. And His presence is with us always.

Because we are joint heirs with Christ, we have all He has. Best of all, we have Him. So in times of stress, remember you have an unlimited resource in God. He is *El Shaddai*, the God of more than enough. He is your help in times of trouble. Yes, there is much you can do to manage or even eliminate stress, but your best resource is God.

CAN YOU RELATE?

All of us can relate to feeling overwhelmed. Sometimes stress is exhilarating. Most times it's exhausting.

Stress is brought to you by life circumstances and attitude. When things go wrong and people let you down, stress is there.

If you've never experienced stress, check your pulse; you are probably dead! So rather than tell you other people's stories, read my "Best-Stressed List" and see if you are in danger of winning this undesirable award.

Dr. Linda's Best-Stressed List

1. Drink as much alcohol as you can to numb pain and avoid life.

2. Use drugs, particularly illegal ones, to escape from life's problems.

3. Run down your body in every way possible. Eat lots of fast foods, stay up late at night and sit around and vegetate.

4. Get yourself into huge financial trouble. Use your credit cards and spend wildly and impulsively. If you like it, just buy it!

5. Whenever there is bad news, assume you will be the next victim. Think about it. Worry about it. Fill your mind with the tragedies of the nightly news.

6. Become a regular complainer, and criticize everything in sight. Make sure you don't let anyone's mistakes pass. Yell, scream and show no mercy.

7. Be a victim of everything and everyone. Make sure you pass around blame as much as you can. Believe you are never at fault for anything.

8. Never make a decision. Since you might make a mistake, don't decide anything. Waver. Agonize.

9. Read into everyone's behavior. They probably don't like you, are trying to compete with you and want you out of the picture. Live in paranoia.

10. Stay away from happy people. They could rub off on you and cause you to cheer up. You have too much to feel bad about and don't need anyone disrupting your unhappy flow.

STRESS, STRESS, STRESS

If this list describes you, it won't take long to become overstressed. Maybe you've crossed the line already, or maybe you relate to too many items on the list. Whatever the case, it's time to break free from overstress. In this book, you will learn how to:

- Understand stress and how it operates in your life

- Recognize different types of stress

- Identify the signs of being over-stressed

- Know biblical guidelines for dealing with stress

- Learn strategies to manage and break free from stress

- Apply stress-free strategies to specific problems

- Live your life in God's peace

BREAKING F R E E

PRAYER FOR YOU

Lord, help me to turn to You to better understand and handle the stress in my life. Amen.

CHAPTER 1

UNDERSTANDING STRESS

Reality is the leading cause of stress amongst those in touch with it.

—JANE WAGNER
(AND LILY TOMLIN)

Stressed out! Burned out! Overwhelmed! Over the edge! Losing it! Yes, 43 percent of us suffer health effects from stress. And did you know that an estimated 70 to 90 percent of all visits to physicians' offices are stress related? Not only is stress considered a work hazard, but it is also linked to the six leading causes of death—heart disease, cancer, lung ailments, accidents, cirrhosis of the liver and suicide.[1]

Stress, however, doesn't have to be negative. Some forms of stress can activate and energize us and make us more productive. Yet at other times, stress can cause a state of fatigue, irritability and depression. Both positive and negative stress must be managed in order to prevent physical, emotional and financial damage.

Stress happens. If you are among the living, it can't be avoided. So what exactly is stress? Sometimes stress is an *event* or the way we *perceive* things. Other times stress is a response to demanding situations. "Stress describes the biological *responses* of an organism to adverse stimuli, either physical, mental or emotional, internal or external, or some combination of these. Such responses can disrupt normal bodily states."[2] In other words, stress is the way our bodies and minds react to change and problems.

When stress is present, our physical bodies react. The brain releases chemicals and hormones, heart rate and blood pressure increase, the immune system is activated, the throat can become dry and tense, the skin becomes cool, clammy or sweaty, and the digestive system shuts down.[3]

The challenge, then, is to face stress without allowing it to overwhelm and seriously impair our thoughts and bodies.

Positive Stress

Do you remember sitting at the top of the roller coaster waiting to dive down a bazillion feet? The feeling of terror was mixed with excitement. Your adrenaline was flowing; you took a deep breath and closed your eyes, and down you plunged. After you put your heart back in your chest, you thought, *Hey, that was great!* And back you went for more. (OK, some of us had to throw up a few times first!)

> *Stress happens. If you are among the living, it can't be avoided.*

Or remember when you prepared for your first piano recital without the music? I do. I was sure I would forget the notes. Of course, the worry and dread that overtook me didn't exactly help my memory. Mom was smiling confidently, and Dad was half-asleep. When it was my turn to play, the piano teacher mispronounced my name, which really boosted my confidence. "Just sit down, back straight, hands on the keys, and play," I coached myself as my sweaty fingers kept slipping off the keys. "You can do this." Amazingly I did. Well, if we don't count the time I totally forgot the piece, burst into tears and left the room.

And how about those college entrance exams? The stress was enough to bring me to my knees and dedicate my life to foreign missions or feeding the poor. Going to Africa (or anywhere for that matter) sounded like a real option once I opened the test booklets and the clock began to tick away.

Who wouldn't count the "I do" for a life-time as stress? For men, this usually tops their "Most Anxious Moments" list. For women, the wedding preparations turn us into raving lunatics. Then we move on to another developmental milestone—the birth of a baby. Yes, it feels as if the baby will never come out and you will be the only woman on earth to never complete the task.

In all of these examples, stress pushed us harder (no birth pun intended!), roused us to action and generally moved us forward. Positive stress comes and goes, like the per-fect houseguest. It makes our lives exciting, fun and challenging. It momentarily taxes our bodies and mental abilities, but we quickly recover and move forward.

NEGATIVE STRESS

When too much stress is experienced, or stress continues over a long period, the positive benefits can turn negative. We may find ourselves stuck in physical exhaustion and emotional despair. We may perceive the situation hopeless with no end in sight.

Negative stress can harm. It is usually easy to identify—death, divorce, imprisonment, poverty, war, disease and so on. You can probably think of several negative stress events or responses to events you've experienced. And perhaps your *thinking* has led you to respond negatively to stress.

> *The important thing to remember is that stress can be both positive and negative.*

The important thing to remember is that stress can be both positive and negative. *Change* is often the initiator of any stress. Other times, stress is caused by the daily hassles of living our lives. Perhaps you are overscheduled, always in a hurry and never have time to do the things you need to do. If so, it's time to slow down and reevaluate your life.

How to Think About Stress in Your Life

It's not the purpose of this book to go into a long and detailed explanation of the biochemical intricacies of stress. I'm not a physician. But as a therapist, I'd like to help you gain a basic understanding in order to make changes and live in peace.

In order to break free, it is important to understand how stress operates in your life. So far, we know that stress can be positive or negative and that both types affect our bodies and minds. We can also determine what *kinds* of stress we face. Are they predictable or unpredictable, major or minor, short-lived or ongoing?

General Categories of Stress

As you begin to think about the stress you currently face, try to identify each stressor by category. Are you dealing with an event, a transition, the environment, a developmental change, a personality trait or your perception of something? You may face multiple stressors at one time.

Stress Categories

1. *Events*. This category includes specific events like death, divorce, diagnosis of disease, a traffic ticket, a broken window, car problems, the Christmas play and more.

2. *Transitions*. A transition is a change from one thing to the next, like a move, job promotion, a fortieth birthday, job change and so on.

3. *The environment*. People who live in crowded urban areas often contend with bad air, crowded streets, traffic, allergies or other factors. Those in the Midwest are subject to tornadoes. Coastal residents have the threat and reality of hurricanes.

Poverty and homelessness are stressful environmental conditions in most cities. And rural people often lack access to services.

4. *Development.* Developmental transitions happen in your individual and family life cycle. Common ones are puberty, marriage, parenting, menopause and retirement. Each has unique stressors that can be positive and negative.

5. *Perceptions.* The way you perceive or think about all of the above creates stress. Obviously if you are a worrier or distrust others, you'll experience more stress. If you are negative and are always looking to support your negative view, you will feel more stressed. Also, perceiving things inaccurately can lead to stress.

6. *Personality.* People who are perfectionists, who need to feel in control, want to please others or constantly compete and worry about their competence are more prone to the effects of stress. If

you are angry, easily frustrated, unorganized or impatient, you experience more stress than others. In other words, personality traits can bring on stress.

The Number of Stressors

Another important question to ask is, "How much stress is operating in my life at one time?" Obviously if you face one or two small problems, you'll cope better than someone with five to six major stressors. Here's an example: A new mom who recently had a hysterectomy and is dealing with elderly parents' health issues while her husband finishes graduate school has much more stress than a new mom without those additional pressures.

When many sources of stress hit at once, it's hard to take. One solution is to eliminate the stress you can. For example, if you have taken on too many responsibilities, learn to say *no* and drop unnecessary tasks now. When stress is self-imposed, you have the power to reduce it. Even when stress isn't self-imposed, you can act to make changes.

Is This a Major or Minor Stress?

It's far easier for most people to cope with small upsets than major ones. For example, families who lost loved ones in the 9/11 terrorist attacks have more to cope with than those of us frustrated by unfriendly bank tellers, rude checkout clerks or a minor car accident.

However, small upsets can be viewed as major sources of stress. It's all in how you perceive the situation. I was driving my kids to school the other day and was stuck in the slow lane behind a truck. The guy behind me was going crazy in his car. I could see him (and read his lips) as he was swearing and waving his fists. He looked like he was about to have a stroke right there in his car. Obviously, for him, the slow traffic was a *major* problem.

Someone who makes a small event like slow drivers a major problem will experience more stress. You may know them as

"Type A" personalities or "worry warts."
Your perceptions and expectations are
important in terms of your response to
stress.

PREDICTABLE OR UNPREDICTABLE STRESS?

Is the stress you experience predictable or
unpredictable? Predictable stress, like the
birth of a baby, is often easier to handle
because there is time to prepare. For example, new parents usually take time off
work, buy supplies ahead of time, organize
family help and support and read books
about baby development. When everything
goes as planned, the stress of a new baby is
one of those positive predictable stresses.

Unpredictable stress throws us for a loop.
In our birth example, a baby who is born
prematurely and spends days in the NIC
(Neo-natal Intensive
Care) Unit creates   *Eliminate the stress*
more stress because   *you can.*
parents have to deal with things unantici-
pated. There is no time to prepare when the
unexpected happens. This unpredictability

makes us more vulnerable to the effects of stress.

ACUTE OR CHRONIC STRESS?

Another important consideration is whether stress is short-lived (acute) or ongoing (chronic). Short-lived stress is usually easier to handle. The reason is that our bodies can recover better and faster. Chronic stress taxes our system and basically wears us out.

Acute stress happens regularly. Usually it includes demands of the recent past or near future—kind of a laundry list of problems such as the telephone repairman who doesn't show up, an assigned work deadline, an attack of the flu in the middle of an important project, an unkind word spoken by a family member, a test or performance evaluation you receive. Acute stress causes emotional disruption and short-lived physical effects. You might feel anxious, tense or worried, have butterflies in your stomach, tense muscles or an upset stomach. But once the stress is over, these symptoms usually disappear.

Chronic or long-term stress causes more problems because it uses up our resources and wears us down over time. Examples of chronic stress are fighting cancer or any long-term illness, living in poverty, interacting with a dysfunctional family, living in an unhappy marriage, stuck in an unsatisfying job or Middle East tensions. An immediate solution

Acute stress causes emotional disruption and short-lived physical effects.

is unforeseen. The stress seems unrelenting. Chronic stress can lead to suicide, violence, heart attack, stroke and other serious problems when coping breaks down or resources are overtaxed.

THE IMPORTANCE OF RESOURCES

I've mentioned "resources" several times now. They are critical when it comes to coping with stress. When you use up more resources than you have, you are in trouble. *Resources are those things that support you and help you cope.* They include relationship support from family, friends, spouse and community; finances; status and power; personality characteristics such as positive optimism, longsuffering and patience; high tolerance for stress; positive attitudes; health; problem-solving skills; a good memory; talents and abilities; organization and more. If you are unsure what your personal resources are, ask a close friend or counselor to help you identify them.

It's a good idea to list them on a piece of paper. You may be surprised by how many resources you have when it comes to dealing with stress. Or you may find that relationship problems, bad habits and negative thinking make you vulnerable to stress. If so, find more resources.

As mentioned earlier, the greatest resource you possess is a personal relationship with Jesus Christ. It is through this intimate relationship that we are sustained through difficulty. And this resource is available to anyone who desires it. It is so powerful that it can counter the lack of other resources.

Without faith and an eternal perspective on this life, it is hard to face stress. Being a

Christian in no way excludes you from stress. In fact, you may even have more if you are persecuted or ridiculed for your faith. However, the promise that God is always with us and will go through any difficulty means we never face life alone. We have His abiding presence. And we have all of His promises to comfort

The greatest resource you possess is a personal relationship with Jesus Christ.

us and bring us a supernatural peace through life's storms. This is truly amazing. He left us to deal with a fallen world, but He prepares us to live in it.

While it is important to be financially, physically and emotionally responsible (and some of you have to work on these areas), it is imperative to plug in to real power. With Christ, not only can we overcome life's difficulties, but we can also be transformed in the process.

BREAKING FREE

PRAYER FOR YOU

Lord, help me understand the role stress plays in my life. I realize I can't live stress free, but I can learn to manage stress and be a good steward of all You have given me. Thank You for sending Your Son and providing me Your presence, comfort and peace no matter what my circumstances.

CHAPTER 2

IDENTIFYING STRESS

Over the years your bodies become walking autobiographies, telling friends and strangers alike of the minor and major stresses of your lives.
—MARILYN FERGUSON

*T*oo many of us feel stressed out but don't know why. We are too stressed to think about it! Consequently we walk around in a daze, unable to act or function well. So it's time to shake off that overwhelmed feeling and start doing something about it. Let's begin by having you identify the stress that personally affects you.

In 1967, two researchers named Holmes and Rahe developed a stress test that ranked forty-three stress-producing events on a scale from 0–100 (100 was the most stressed).[1] If you experience many of these, you could be at risk for health and mental health problems.

Take this classic stress test.[2] Just check the items that apply to you. Then, add all the numbers assigned to each item you checked to give you a total score. Your score is an indication of how at risk you are for developing a stress-related illness. A high score doesn't mean you will become ill, only that you are at risk.

BREAKING F R E E
MENTAL HEALTH FACT

Social Readjustment Rating Scale

Death of a spouse	100	____
Divorce	73	____
Marital separation	65	____
Jail term	63	____
Death of close family member	63	____
Personal injury or illness	53	____
Marriage	50	____
Fired from work	47	____

Marital reconciliation	45	_____
Retirement	45	_____
Change in family member's health	44	_____
Pregnancy	40	_____
Sex difficulties	39	_____
Addition to family	39	_____
Business readjustment	39	_____
Change in financial status	38	_____
Death of close friend	37	_____
Change to different line of work	36	_____
Change in number of marital arguments	35	_____
Mortgage or loan over $10,000	31	_____
Foreclosure of mortgage or loan	30	_____
Change in work responsibilities	29	_____
Son or daughter leaving home	29	_____
Trouble with in-laws	29	_____

Outstanding personal achievement	28	____
Spouse begins or stops work	26	____
Starting or finishing school	26	____
Change in living conditions	25	____
Revision of personal habits	24	____
Trouble with boss	23	____
Change in work hours, conditions	20	____
Change in residence	20	____
Change in schools	20	____
Change in recreational habits	19	____
Change in religious activities	19	____
Change in social activities	18	____
Mortgage or loan under $10,000	17	____
Change in sleeping habits	16	____

Change in number of family gatherings	15	____
Change in eating habits	15	____
Vacation	13	____
Christmas season	12	____
Minor violation of the law	11	____

TOTAL SCORE ____

SCORING

- Less than 150—means you have a 30 percent chance of developing a stress-related illness.

- 150–299—means you have a 50 percent chance.

- Over 300—means you have an 80 percent chance.

~~~~~~

Keep in mind that if you have a low stress tolerance, scores below 150 can cause problems as well. Use this score to give you an idea about your stress level. For example, I experienced stress this past year because I made a major move across country. My score was 464! Fortunately, I'm not ill and know how to mediate the effects of high stress. You can learn to do the same.

I have included a stress chart on pages 24–25 to help you identify the current stress you face. Use the stress scale as a guide.

Take a look at the first column, and list "Stressors" that affect you right now. Think about the categories discussed in chapter one and those items you checked on the stress scale. Do you have stress from an event, a transition, the environ-ment, development, your perception of something or someone, or from your per-sonality and character traits? As you think about those categories, write down any stress that comes to mind. For example, your list may include items like these:

- Financial debt
- Colicky baby
- Boss pressure to bring up sales
- Critical mother-in-law
- No one seems to like me at school.
- No time for myself

- Gaining weight
- Want everything to be perfect

Remember that positive stress is still stress. Include any recent changes in your list.

Next, for each stress listed, write whether the stress is predictable or unpredictable (column 2), whether you feel it is major or minor (column 3) and acute or chronic (column 4). Predictable stress is usually easier to deal with because responses can be planned and practiced in advance. Major stress is more debilitating than minor stress, and people rebound more easily from acute (short-lived) stress than chronic (long-term) stress. So, look at your list and count how many stressors are unpredictable, major and chronic. If the number is high, you are more at risk for emotional and physical problems.

Finally, write out any resources that might help you deal with stress, such as family support, finances, faith, a forgiving heart, influence or assertiveness skills. Remember that resources are those things that help you cope and bring support. They

SAMPLE CHART

Stressor	Predictable/ Unpredictable	Major/ Minor	Acute/ Chronic	Resources to deal with it
Need to make this month's sales quota	Predictable	Major	Acute	Good contacts, sales pending, savings, supportive wife
Ill child	Unpredictable	Minor	Acute	Parents can baby-sit and help, health insurance, prayer

		Stress Chart for your use		
Stressor	Predictable/ Unpredictable	Major/ Minor	Acute/ Chronic	Resources to deal with it

include more than just money, power, accomplishment and attractiveness. Your faith, trust in God, intimate relationship, prayer and knowledge of Scripture are extremely helpful during stressful times. Don't minimize the importance of these.

FIVE LIFESTYLE QUESTIONS TO EVALUATE STRESS IN YOUR LIFE

Your lifestyle can help you deal with stress, or it can add to stress. So let's do a quick evaluation of your *lifestyle*.

1. Do I have effective ways of relaxing?

We all need down time. Therefore, identify ways to relax and rejuvenate your body and mind. Relaxing should be a regular, practiced part of your life. You need balance in all things. Even God rested on the seventh day! Relaxation keeps stress from building up, and it provides an avenue for tension release.

2. Are you exercising regularly?

So many of us know the importance of exercising, but we don't do it. The benefits of exercise are enormous. Exercise can reduce muscle tension and frustration in addition to providing a host of medical helps. So why don't we exercise regularly? Either we don't have a moment to fit it into our day, or we don't enjoy it. The solution is to make time and pick something you like— bike riding, dancing, skating, basketball, tennis, skiing, walking, Ping-Pong—anything that gets you active and off that couch.

3. How sensibly do you eat?

Do you skip meals, eat burgers in the car while talking on your cell phone and find yourself at the drive-through regularly? Decrease your caffeine intake (caffeine can trigger panic), reduce salt, eat more organic and less processed foods, and eat foods that give energy and staying power. Get the vitamins and supplements you need, particularly vitamins B, C and calcium for women.

4. How well do you manage your time?

Learn time management and ways to maximize your efforts. Some people have to learn to move things along; others need to slow down and do things correctly. You have only so much time in a day, so it is important to learn to prioritize and be realistic about goals.

5. Are you getting sleep?

This sounds like a simple question, but so many clients I see have terrible sleep habits. It is important to go to bed at a regular time and get into a sleep routine. This means start winding down a few hours before you go to sleep.

Take a minute and begin to ask these questions. Then, work on making simple but important lifestyle changes.

BREAKING FREE

PRAYER FOR YOU

Lord, teach me to make the lifestyle changes that will reduce stress and allow me to relax more. Amen.

CHAPTER 3

BIBLICAL GUIDELINES
FOR STRESS

You will guard him and keep him in perfect and constant peace whose mind [both its inclination and its character] is stayed on You, because he commits himself to You, leans on You, and hopes confidently in You.

—ISAIAH 26:3, AMP

One of the many benefits of being a Christian is that you have a relationship with God who hears and wants to be involved in your life. In fact, He desires to be intimate with you. Take Him up on this desire, and get to know Him. When you do, you will find Him to be the greatest resource of all when it comes to managing stress.

In Romans, Paul reminds us that our old

man was crucified with Christ. We are no longer slaves to our old nature. But our sinful nature likes to raise its ugly head and is prone to worry, anxiety, pride, deception and independence. Often, we try to handle life on our own. When stress mounts, we become overwhelmed because we rely on our own power and not the power of the Holy Spirit.

To manage stress, first decide if you are doing things to bring stress into your life. Not everything that happens to us is a result of living in an evil world. We are human and capable of making mistakes, of acting unwisely and sinning. We often bring unnecessary stress into our lives by the choices we make. So, take inventory. Make better choices. Make changes where you can.

If you struggle with addiction, sexual sin or are out of balance with work and prideful ambition, you are adding stress to your life. Repent of these things, and get help. Take responsibility for your choices and actions. Line up your behavior with biblical instruction. This is one of the best ways to eliminate self-imposed stress.

When followed, God's directives for living bring us to a place of supernatural peace. How else could Paul and others face persecution and still rejoice?

Second, we need to stop relying solely on our own abilities to get us through tough times. I'm all for avoiding stressful situations by using my mind and abilities, but to be totally self-reliant is very American and wrong. Positive thinking is godly, but it is not the end-all to every stressful situation. We are to be dependent on God in all things, recognizing that He is the

Don't fight daily stress alone. You have a champion who wants to head the battle.

source of our strength and the strength of our lives. Act as if the situation depends on you, but know that God is in control. Ultimately we should be dependent on Him.

When we depend on God to champion our cause, fight our battles, deliver or walk us through the fire, we are relieved from carrying the weight of such burdens. He tells us in Matthew 11:30 that His yoke is easy and His burden light. Don't fight daily stress alone. You have a champion who wants to head the battle.

Accept the fact that not all situations in our lives resolve quickly. There are times when we suffer, struggle and wonder why God isn't taking us out of a problem. Sometimes we can't understand why something is happening—we can only trust God to walk us through it. Difficulties often bring growth, spiritual learning, an opportunity to apply godly principles and kingdom living. Christians often refer to these times as *refining fires* or *pruning*. Stressful times are moments to practice what you know to be true of God. Align your behavior, and conform to His image. Renew your mind. Stand in faith. Confess His promises. Conform to His image.

Keep in mind that disaster falls on the just and unjust. But God promises His presence to those who believe. You are not alone even though you may feel alone. You serve a God of love and compassion. He will help you get through this rough time. Also remember that you serve the God of the impossible. Even when it seems as if there is no hope, God can act.

Stress provides an opportunity to draw closer to God. It also gives fellow Christians a chance to be supportive and act as a loving body. During stressful times, most of us are more open to change and seek God. This can be a good thing and can strengthen your walk. God says He is our refuge, but you won't find His refuge if you don't go to Him. Let Him wrap you in His loving arms and give you the peace that passes all understanding. You are sheltered in His arms.

Relationship with God brings the soundness of mind we so desperately need on a day-to-day basis. My encouragement to you is to stop trying to do things in your own power and seek God for direction and peace. There is much He wants to do for you if you let Him.

USE THE GUIDELINES

Use these biblical guidelines in times of stress. Look up and read each of the Bible verses listed.

Don't rely on your own power to get through. Cry out to God, and He will hear and help you.

- 2 Samuel 22:7
- 2 Chronicles 15:4
- 2 Chronicles 20:9
- Psalm 18:6
- Psalm 55:17
- Psalm 107:28

When you are tempted to worry and feel anxiety mounting, remember to cast your cares on Jesus.

- Matthew 6:25
- Matthew 6:34
- Psalm 139:23
- Psalm 91:5
- Romans 13:3

Use the biblical prescription for worry and anxiety related to stress.

So much of stress relates to feeling out of control. In reality, we aren't in control anyway. God is. He sees the big picture, and nothing happens away from His watchful eye. It's rare that things go according to our plans. Most of living is a rough and bumpy road. Read Philippians

4:6–9, and then learn to apply it to your stress situations.

According to this scripture, first thank God. You don't have to thank Him for the stress you are experiencing; just thank Him for who He is. Next, talk to God through prayer and tell Him your request. Verse 8 instructs us to meditate on things that are noble, pure, lovely, of good report, virtuous and praiseworthy, and God will give us peace (v. 9). The result is a peace we can't understand in the natural but one that guards our hearts and mind.

Meditate on the Word.

This is what the Bible calls "renewing your mind."

Whenever stress seems to rear its ugly head, remember your greatest resource—God! He wants to help you, be with you and bring you peace!

PRAYER FOR YOU

Lord, I'm asking You to take this _____ (fill in the stress) and help me deal with it according to Your Word. Help me change any problem that may be adding stress to my life because of bad choices. Next, I want to bring my burdens and cares to You and stop trying to be so self-reliant. Finally, I want to have Your perfect peace, so I am praying to be anxious about nothing. Fill me with Your peace, and give me what I need to face my life challenges.

Chapter 4

Break-Free Strategies for Stress

I am convinced that life is 10 percent what happens to me and 90 percent how I react to it.
—Charles Swindoll

*I*n order to break free from stress, pay attention to your physical body. Look for signs of stress (chapter two). It is also a good idea to get a physical from your physician in order to rule out any illness or disease that may have similar symptoms to being overstressed. Then, try these break-free strategies. If you still find you are overstressed, see a mental health professional who can guide you.

Successful coping with stress involves using the resources you have. *First, look at your resource list*. What do you have available to help you (tangible things like support, money, time, power, status, influence or more internal things like faith in God, confidence, patience and prayer)? How will you use what's available? What strengths do you have that will help the situation? This varies from person to person.

Second, use a coping strategy. Basically there are two major strategies:

1. Take direct action to change the stressful situation.

2. Rethink the situation. Usually this involves coming to terms with the positive side of stress—what can you learn, and how can you grow?

A combination of both strategies can be used as well.

Here's an example. Debbie was constantly upset by the critical nature of her stepfather. Her mother remarried, and Debbie still lived at home. Debbie never liked her stepfather because he rarely had a kind word. Most of his comments were critical and demeaning. Debbie was stressed living at home. She couldn't stand the stepfather's constant complaints.

Debbie could do a number of things based on the strategies above. She could talk directly to her stepfather about his behavior, but she didn't think this would change things. She could move out. After all, she was an adult, and her mother made the choice to marry this guy. If Debbie didn't like his behavior, she could get her own place.

The situation actually prompted Debbie to rethink her growing dependency on her mom. While she wasn't fond of the new stepdad, his presence made her realize her need for more independence. In Debbie's case, she acted (moved out) and chose to rethink her situation (she needed more independence). She chose not to let the stress continue to build. Instead she made changes and used her resources to move out.

Most people learn coping strategies from their families. They watch how family members handle times of stress and model their behavior. However, you can learn new ways to cope. If you have learned dysfunctional family coping styles, you are not doomed. Just recognize that those strategies don't work and that new behavior and thinking are needed.

PHYSICAL STRATEGIES TO REDUCE STRESS

Stress affects people differently. Some carry stress in their physical bodies. Physical symptoms emerge, and tense muscles result. Others are more stressed because of their thoughts. They worry and become anxious. Some people do both! For those of you who feel *body* tension, use physical techniques to relax your muscles.

Deep muscle relaxation

If you tend to carry stress around in your physical body, if you are prone to tension in your head (eyes, throat, jaw) or in your neck, shoulders and back, here is a technique you can learn and practice. It is called deep muscle relaxation.

Deep muscle relaxation is based on the idea that tensing a muscle and then releasing it produces a state of relaxation. So if you take the muscle groups in your body and practice tensing all of them, and then releasing the tension, you should feel quite relaxed. You don't have to tense so hard that you hurt yourself! Just clench, tighten, make a fist, etc., stop the tension and concentrate on the next fifteen seconds of relaxation.

Here's how you practice. Find a comfortable and quiet place. Start with one muscle and tense it. Wait a few seconds (study the tension), release it and feel the relaxation (about fifteen seconds). Repeat this with various muscle groups, including your stomach, head (eyes, mouth, jaw), triceps, back, biceps— all parts of your body, making sure no tension creeps in when you practice.

The next time you feel tension in your body, try deep muscle relaxation.

Concentrate on each muscle and clear your head of other thoughts. You can even purchase relaxation tapes in which someone coaches you through the exercise.

You should practice for about twenty minutes a day. It usually takes about twenty to thirty minutes to go through all the muscle groups and become completely relaxed. I like to have people practice first thing in the morning and right before bed at night.

This way, your day starts calm and ends the same. Practicing at night also helps you fall asleep. This is a way to relax your body without using drugs and alcohol.

The next time you feel tension in your body, try deep muscle relaxation. You can train your body to relax. It works!

Take a deep breath and relax.

Here's another way to practice relaxation: Take a deep breath and relax! Keep in mind that the opposite of tension and stress is relaxation. Relaxation comes in many forms. Sometimes it has to be learned and practiced. You have to teach your body how to relax.

When you are tense, breathing often becomes short and rapid. It tends to originate in the chest. Some people even hyperventilate, which can lead to panic. Breathing should come from the abdomen, not the chest. If you are unsure, place your hand on your abdomen, take a breath and see if your hand moves. If you don't feel an in-and-out motion, chances are you are breathing from your chest and throat.

When you concentrate on taking deep,

slow breaths, you supply more oxygen to the brain and muscle system. You stimulate the parasympathetic nervous system, which calms you. Taking deep breaths can help clear your mind, too. Try to concentrate on your body. Try to inhale slowly through the nose, and let the air go down low. Pause and slowly exhale through your nose or mouth.

Do this over and over, about ten times. When you practice deep breathing three or four times a day, you will catch yourself breathing incorrectly and teach your body to correct the breathing. The more often you sense stress in your body, the more you can apply this technique. So the next time you feel tension creeping into your body, take a deep breath and relax!

Get support.

Mary could barely lift her head after the chemotherapy. Slouching in her sofa, trying to ward off the nausea, she glanced at the inside of her house. Tears filled her eyes. Two of her best friends had spent their day cleaning her house. They knew how ill Mary felt after chemotherapy treatments and wanted to relieve some of the stress related to caring for Mary's family.

John was under pressure to make his deadline at the newspaper. When he stared at the sheer volume of work left unfinished, his heart started to pound. The task was impossible, but then Dan showed up. Dan canceled his plans for the night. He knew the pressure John was under regarding the deadline. He wanted to help. John breathed a huge sigh of relief.

Jennifer didn't know how she would take her elderly mother to her doctor's appointment. Three of her babysitters were unavailable, and she had no one to watch the children. Her neighbor stopped by and noticed Jennifer's distress. "Is there anything I can do to help—maybe watch the kids for a few hours while you take your mom to the doctor?"

The more social support you have, the better you'll fare when it comes to managing stress.

All three of these people were less stressed because of the willingness of others to lend a helping hand. The more social support you have, the better you'll fare when it comes to managing stress. Social support, whether given by family, friends or even strangers, is a stress reducer. Support buffers us in times of high stress. It helps us face difficulty and still function in our lives.

Social support involves the perception that you are being cared for and loved, that you can count on others and that you are valued regardless of your achievements. It is an established fact that the lack of social support can lead to psychological problems.

Social support makes you feel less isolated. All people have a need for ongoing care, recognition, affection and belonging. Ongoing support is a benefit regardless of the level of stress experienced.

Social support also helps you avoid negative life events by providing information and opportunities. For example, in times of financial stress, you may feel less strain because family members are supportive and provide temporary aid.

The most important benefits of social support are improved health and psychological well-being. When people reach out to lend a hand or are with you during difficult times, it really makes a difference.

The next time you see someone stressed out, offer to help—wash her dishes, take the kids for an hour, run an errand, send a dinner, be available to listen, give comfort or offer your assistance. It not only benefits the person who needs it, but you too will feel good about what you've done.

Regulate your sleep schedule.

As I mentioned earlier, lifestyle changes are helpful. If possible, try to bring regularity to your schedule, particularly when it comes to sleep and wake-up times. Set a time to go to sleep each night and wake up each morning. You can reduce stress by regulating your body clock. Usually it takes about three weeks to make a change, so don't give up quickly. If you can't sleep, try reading a book or thinking of something calming and pleasant. Better yet, pray quietly as you try to fall asleep.

If you are a shift worker, try to stay on the same shift for a period of time. Regulate your sleep pattern as well. Traveling throws off your body clock, too.

When you arrive at your destination, try to stay up later and adjust to the schedule of the new time zone.

Make environmental changes when possible.

As I mentioned, the environment can cause stress. So when you can, make changes such as these: Work by a window so you have daylight exposure; avoid allergies; use ergonomic keyboards and chairs that support your back; take frequent breaks from a sitting job and walk around; avoid secondhand smoke. Think of ways you can eliminate sources of stress in your environment.

Change your diet and exercise.

As noted in chapter two, reevaluate your eating habits. Stop skipping meals, and eat healthy food. Take a multivitamin. Reduce sugar, caffeine, tobacco and alcohol. Try to exercise at least three times a week for twenty minutes. Walking is a great way to begin.

Cut out activities.

So many people I know are overstressed

because they are involved in too many activities. Reduce the number of social, sports, work and church events if you find yourself on the run with no down time. You and your children don't have to be involved in everything. Say *no* to overload, and give your family a rest.

Reevaluate your priorities. Do you spend time on things that are unimportant but have little time to do necessary tasks? Do you waste time by watching too much TV or sitting at your computer? Are you at work too many hours because family relationships are much harder and less satisfying? Are you so busy that you have no quiet time to spend with God?

> *Little changes add up to big differences. Big changes bring long-lasting results.*

Spend time in worship.

I am convinced that transformation comes as we sit in the presence of God. Worship gives our undivided attention to God. Spend time singing, praising and loving God alone and in corporate worship with a vibrant church body. You were created to worship God. In His presence are fullness of joy, peace, refreshment and love. Your life will change, and stress will fade.

Begin with small changes.

It's unrealistic to eliminate all stress from our lives, but we can change our response to stress. Little changes add up to big differences. Big changes bring long-lasting results.

Next time stress has you wishing you could fly to a new planet, stay on this one and de-stress. Here are small changes you can make that can reduce stress in your life. Then add your own ideas to this list.

BREAKING FREE

MENTAL HEALTH FACT

Take Steps to Reduce Your Stress

- Make copies of important papers.
- Make duplicate car and home keys.
- Take a bubble bath.
- Listen to music or read a poem.
- Clean one thing.
- Choose clothes the night before.
- Go on a picnic.

- Make needed appointments.
- Write it down.
- Smile and laugh more often.
- Hold a baby.
- Sit under the stars.
- Read a great book.
- Get a bouquet of fresh flowers.
- Don't wait; do it today.
- Go to a movie—and eat popcorn.
- Get a massage or facial.
- Praise someone and praise God.
- Take a deep breath and relax.
- Take a nature walk.
- Get a pet—and get unconditional love.
- Repair broken things.
- Break big tasks into smaller jobs.
- Ask for help when you need it.

Determine to make a small change every week.

COGNITIVE STRATEGIES FOR STRESS REDUCTION

If stress originates more from your *thoughts*, you need *cognitive* strategies to help you relax. Two good ones are visualizing peaceful scenes and meditation. Now don't get crazy on me and think I am about to embark on some New Age quest for serenity. I'm not talking about repeating mantras or engaging in transcendental meditation.

Christians can meditate and visualize. The Bible even directs us to do so:

> Whatever things are true, whatever things are noble, whatever things are just, whatever things are pure, whatever things are lovely, whatever things are of good report, if there is any virtue and if there is anything praiseworthy— meditate on these things.
> —PHILIPPIANS 4:8, NKJV

All you do is focus your mind on things that bring peace and a sense of well-being. Think about God's intense love for you. Meditation is prayer. When we pray and spend time with our heavenly Father, we feel better and less stressed. We have a Dad who promises to take care of us and meet our needs. If that doesn't lessen your stress, nothing will.

I know that visualization and meditation have a bad rap because they are usually associated with New Age and Eastern religions. But Christians can meditate on God. Think about His promises and experience His love. When you do, tension leaves, and you feel refreshed in spirit and mind.

When you feel stressed and tense, you can also visualize yourself in a quiet peaceful place. This is calming. Some people like to imagine themselves on a sunny beach with a gentle breeze, the smell of the ocean, clear skies and water. Other people find a mountain cabin in the snow to be a quiet calming place. Still others imagine basking eternally in the presence of God. It doesn't matter what scene you choose; just think of something peaceful and try to engage all your senses in the scene. All this does is distract your anxious thoughts to a place of peace.

We have a Dad who promises to take care of us and meet our needs. If that doesn't lessen your stress, nothing will.

The idea behind meditation and visualization is to calm your anxiety and bring peace. We know that *true* peace comes from having a personal relationship with Jesus

Christ. Remember His promise to keep us in perfect peace if we keep our mind stayed on Him (Isa. 26:3). God is the giver of peace and serenity. Think about Him—His goodness, His love and all He has done for you.

Learn to say no.

Too many of us take on too much because we don't say *no*. We are afraid to set limits; we don't feel we have the right. Or we need to please others and want to be loved for what we do. We may even think that we have to be super human and do it all! Time to turn in your cape! Learn to say *no* and not feel guilty. You'll reduce the stress in your life.

"Sure, I'll cook for the spaghetti dinner." "Yes, I can baby-sit your children for the day." "Yes, I can chair another committee." "Since no one else will volunteer, I guess I'll do it." Do you ever find yourself saying these things and then realize you've taken on too much? You've committed to doing more than you can realistically handle. As a result, you are stressed and kicking yourself for not saying *no*.

Saying *no* to things requires assertiveness.

Assertiveness is behavior that falls somewhere in the middle of giving in and aggressiveness. It is not giving in to the wants of others or keeping silent and expecting people to read your mind. It is also not yelling at people and demanding your way. It is a practiced skill that helps you manage stress. Contrary to popular thought, you don't have to be angry to be assertive. In fact, I prefer you stay calm.

There are two parts involved in being assertive: 1) Know what you want, and 2) say it. One of the reasons we don't practice being assertive is because we don't know what we want. We are wishy-washy, unsure and undefined. We allow others to manipulate us into doing things, and then we feel resentful because we have too much to do. Or we feel guilty and don't believe we have the right to speak up. We ask, "Who am I to say no?"

You are someone important. You are also responsible for managing the stress that comes your way. When you can do something about stress, take the initiative—speak up! Know what you want and take a reasonable position. Do not feel guilty at setting limits. Reduce stress by taking control where and when you can.

Speak up and let your voice be heard. When you address problems as they occur, you won't build up anger and hold on to things that can grow into resentment, leading to depression, anxiety and eating disorders. Many of my female patients have to be taught

Reduce stress by taking control where and when you can.

how to be assertive because it is a skill they've never learned and one that must be practiced.

The benefits from speaking up are improved physical and psychological health. Your relationships will improve, and you will better manage stress. In addition, you will gain respect from people. They may not like your stance, but they will respect you for taking one.

Laugh.

If you could have one of the best antidotes for stress, would you take it? If I told you it was something you could easily access and was free, would you want it? If I raved about how this one thing does everything from decreasing the risk of heart attack to stimulating the immune system, would you order it? Well, get ready, because it's something you already have—at least I hope you have it. It's humor!

Now if you don't have a sense of humor, go get one. Read joke books, listen to comedy and learn to laugh at funny things. You are probably taking life too seriously and need to laugh at yourself and others at least once in awhile.

My private practice group used to kid me that I wasn't doing therapy with my clients. They couldn't hear behind my soundproof walls, but laughter permeated my doorway. What was going on in those therapy sessions that was so funny? Let me assure you, we were dealing with painful and difficult subjects, but I always found some way to bring humor into the mix. Why? Because I know what I am telling you now—humor decreases stress.

A merry heart does good, like a medicine, but a broken spirit dries the bones.

—PROVERBS 17:22, NKJV

Humor is a self-care tool that fosters a positive and hopeful attitude. Humor releases emotions and stimulates the immune system. Humor takes a stressful condition and turns it into a challenge. Humor defuses stress and makes it easier to look at a situation and do something about it. Humor is fun. It feels good to laugh, and it does wonders for your physical body.

I'm not suggesting you laugh off serious matters in your life. I don't want you to deny or avoid problems. I'm simply saying that maintaining a sense of

Humor defuses stress and makes it easier to look at a situation and do something about it.

humor helps during serious times. For example, my mother just called. She was lamenting the number of family and friends ill with serious conditions. But then she injected a humorous thought, "You know, we need to have lots of volunteers at the hospital (she volunteers at the hospital) because we never know who will be able to help and who will be in the beds." We both started laughing.

My mom's ability to laugh and make jokes helps relieve stress. She's not joking at inappropriate times or making fun of people. She laughs at herself, the situation and the craziness of life. Humor is a release from the tension of the stress.

Next time you feel stressed, try to laugh. Take a different perspective and give humor a try. Rent a silly movie. Tell a joke. Tickle someone. Play a crazy game. It just might make you a healthier person!

Become a problem solver.

One of the reasons you may feel stressed is because you aren't very good at solving problems. When you run up against an obstacle, you panic, hyperventilate or fall apart. Immediately you think there is no solution or way to resolve the issue. These responses cause you to feel stressed out.

Be a Good Problem Solver

One way to combat stress is to become a
good problem solver. When a problem
comes your way:

- *Define the problem.* Get a clear
  definition in your head as to what
  the actual difficulty may be. If you
  define the problem, you'll know
  what you need to change.

- *How often or how long is it happening?* Measure the number of
  times the problem occurs or the
  length of time it goes on. This
  way you will have an accurate
  count or duration of the problem. This is important because
  you need to measure change.

- *Do something.* Time to intervene.
  Instead of responding the way
  you always do, or in a way that
  doesn't promote change, try a
  new strategy. Stop doing the thing
  that doesn't work and try a new
  tactic. You can experiment until
  you find something that works.

- *Evaluate how well things are going.* If you have a clear definition of the problem, measure how much of a problem it is and then do something, you can see if the behavior gets better or worse, happens less or more. If your husband is taking out the trash two out of three weeks and he never did it before, you've made progress. Change is usually a step-by-step process that requires lots of encouragement.

- *If what you are doing doesn't work, try another tactic.* The secret here is not to panic or give up. You tried something, and it didn't work. Try something else. Talk to other people—a counselor or family members—and get input if you need it. Just because you don't see a solution doesn't mean there isn't one. There is always a way. Remember this is also a promise from God. He makes a way where there is no way, so don't panic or give up.

Practice problem solving. It will boost

your confidence and reduce stress. Next time you encounter stress, say, "I can deal with this. It's just a matter of finding the right solution and trusting God to help me."

BREAKING ✒ FREE

PRAYER FOR YOU

Lord, help me change my actions and thoughts when it comes to handling stress. There are a number of ways I can change my lifestyle and respond differently to stress situations. I want to face stress with Your confidence and practice new ways to behave. Empower me to make necessary changes.

CHAPTER 5

APPLICATIONS TO COMMON STRESS SITUATIONS

I'm living so far beyond my income that we may almost be said to be living apart.

— E. E. CUMMINGS

Now let's take the physical and mental strategies for reducing stress and apply them to some common stress situations.

JOB STRESS

More Americans are working harder and longer hours just to maintain their standard of living. The price paid is enormous—social life and family life are disrupted, and physical health and psychological health are compromised. According to Steve Sauter, Ph.D., chief of the applied psychological and ergonomics branch of NIOSH (National Institute for Occupational Safety and Health), more jobs have been lost in the past few years than in the two previous decades.[1]

Are downsizing and wage inequality sources of job stress? You bet. People fear losing their jobs and worry about their performances. Too many leave their employment feeling drained and used up. Obviously this leaves little to give to others, particularly family.

Competing in the global market has brought change to American industry. Some would say the biggest change is an unequal distribution of wealth and income. Consequently people work harder just to maintain. And many find themselves always behind and stressed.

What results is an overall sense of loss of control and hopelessness about the future. This is stressful. So what can you do to manage job stress?

Managing Job Stress

- *Recognize the changes.* Companies are downsizing, and global markets make competition for jobs more intense. Change is inevitable, and you need to be ready for it.

- *Don't panic if you are laid off.* God is your provider—not any one company or person. Be faithful in your response to the situation, and trust God to lead you to the next job. Do all you can to find it, and depend on God to act on your behalf.

- *Get a quality education.* People who are college educated do better in this economy. Go to a technology school and develop specific skills that are marketable.

- *Be a good steward of all you have.* Don't spend beyond your means or go into debt. Put aside savings for difficult times.

- *Maximize your work time.* Don't waste time on unimportant things. Get a clear description of what is expected and how you will be evaluated.

- *Be of integrity on the job.* If you read the Scriptures, it is clear God wants to bless you and to provide. Line up your life in accordance to God's Word, be strong in your faith and believe what God says about finances— act according to His principles.

- *Understand what you can and cannot change.* Work on the "can" part.

- *Practice stress management skills.* Leave the job at the job, and give full attention to your family, spouse and your physical, emotional and spiritual health.

- *Maintain a sense of humor.* Humor relieves stress and can help you enjoy the workplace.

PREGNANCY STRESS

Did you know that the way you deal with stress during pregnancy could be related to the way your baby develops in the womb? That's right. If you have stress and anxiety during pregnancy, you may have an early delivery and a baby with low birth weight. But if you think optimistically during pregnancy, the outcome is better. Optimism, it appears, is a predictor of birth weight, and stress is related to time of delivery. These are the conclusions of researchers who presented data at the 1999 Annual Convention of the American Psychological Association (APA) in Boston.

These findings were based on studies conducted by Christine Dunkel-Schetter, Ph.D. of the University of California-Los Angeles and Ann Marie Yali, Ph.D. and her colleagues at the University of Pittsburgh, as well as Marci Lobel, Ph.D. and colleagues at State University of New York at Stonybrook and summarized in the October 1999 issue of the *APA Monitor*.[2]

According to the studies, women who were highly stressed during pregnancy were four times more likely to deliver premature babies than women who experienced little stress. A hormone known as CRH was used as a measure of stress. What the researchers found was that this hormone was higher at different times during pregnancy for women who delivered prematurely.

The study points out that it was not stressful events that affected birth outcomes but the *way women responded to those events*. If you are highly anxious about pregnancy, this may increase your risk for early delivery. Early delivery is associated with low birth rates.

> *If you believe in God, you have reason to be optimistic about the outcome of any life event.*

The good news is that holding positive expectations or optimism about birth and delivery appears to affect the body positively. Optimism was associated with low stress. Women who were optimistic believed they had control over the outcome of pregnancy.

So what can we learn from these findings? Positive thinking pays off in pregnancy as it does in many areas of life. Although the studies are uncertain as to whether stress levels or positive thinking is more important, chances are you'll benefit from managing stress and staying positive about the outcome of your pregnancy.

If you believe in God, you have reason to be optimistic about the outcome of any life event. We can call on God to help us deal with stress and know that He is ultimately in control of all things. Knowing that He walks with us through any difficulty is reassuring and stress reducing. Stay positive, because you serve a great God who is always ready and willing to help you.

Becoming Parents

The transition to parenthood, even when desired, is not easy for most couples. We know from previous research that marriages are vulnerable following the birth of a baby. Marital satisfaction usually decreases. Couples face more conflict and usually have less positive communication. The question, then, is this: What helps couples prevent this normal developmental change from becoming so stressful?

Researchers Shapiro and Gottman attempted to find out by studying a group of couples who did and did not have children during the first six years of marriage. What they found reinforced previous research—wives who had children reported less marital satisfaction than wives who did not become parents. The lowered satisfaction rates for over half the wives occurred a year after birth. For a small percentage, satisfaction decreased two years post-birth.[3]

Husbands who had children were also less satisfied with their marriages compared to those who did not have children. However, the difference between the two groups of husbands was not significant.[4]

The researchers also studied the group of couples who became parents but remained stable or increased their marital satisfaction. What was different about these couples? What was it that helped buffer the stress of having a new baby?

What they found was interesting. Marital friendship was key and included these two things: 1) Spouses had a level of awareness about their partner, his/her life and the couple relationship. 2) Husbands admired and were fond of their wives. Marital friendship seemed to ward off the stress of transition to parenthood.[5]

So if you want to buffer your marital relationship from stress, build your friendship. Focus on things you admire and respect about your spouse. Get to know your spouse's interests, go on dates, talk, have fun together and enjoy each other's company.

Like most friendships, the more time you spend getting to know the person intimately, the deeper the friendship can go. And in marriage, close friendship has a positive effect on countering stress.

Mom Stress

Mom stands for *Mother on the Move*. You wake up at 6:30 A.M. and feed the baby. The two preschoolers, Jack and Jill, wake up. The baby cries. Jill needs her bottom wiped, and Jack has just spilled his milk trying to be Mom's big boy helper. The baby is still screaming. Jill's out of the bathroom and fell on the step. Now she's screaming. Jack, the helper, is dragging her to the "bandage place." The baby stops crying, and you reach down and place the bandage on Jill's scraped knee. For one moment, everyone is silent. You take a deep breath, and it starts again. Jack is jumping up and down yelling, "The baby has spit up all over Mommy's clothes." He seems to be enjoying this! You look at your watch. You've only been up for an hour! Twenty-three more to go! Mom stress is a way of life.

You probably don't know whether to laugh or cry if this is your life. I suggest you laugh because humor helps with stress. Mom stress is a part of mothering. There never seems to be enough of us to go around. By the end of the day, sleep is our only friend.

We give so much of ourselves that we often don't pay attention to our own bodies' need for revitalization.

Being a mom is highly rewarding, but let's admit it—it's also stressful. Moms play multiple roles in a day—cook, taxi driver, homework monitor, nurse, emotional soother and so on. We run from thing to thing, never really having the time to complete anything well. We give so much of ourselves that we often don't pay attention to our own bodies' need for revitalization.

Don't forget that under every mom is a woman in hiding. Find her, and let her out once in awhile. She'll help relieve mom stress.

MARITAL STRESS

Tom and Mary are in the middle of a financial crisis. Both are having difficulty coping with the stress. Mary wants to talk every night when Tom comes home from work. All day she has been thinking about their credit and the bills they owe. She is sure there is no way out of their current problems, and she repeats her doom and gloom predictions to Tom.

Tom loves his wife, but he can't stand her constant chatter about the finances. He's aware of the problems and is trying to remedy the situation the best he can. He too feels highly stressed. It doesn't help him to talk about the same issues over and over. He finds himself reaching for a beer and staring blankly at the TV for a few hours of escape.

Tom and Mary represent many couples coping with stress. If you've ever lived with someone of the opposite sex, you know that men and women cope differently. Women want to talk about problems. To the frustration of many women, men are less likely to do so.

Stress is a part of all of our lives. The goal is to manage it so it doesn't manage you.

In fact, Susan Nolen-Hoeksema, Ph.D., from the University of Michigan, presented a study at the 1999 Annual Convention of the American Psychological Association about the way men and women cope with negative situations. Dr. Hoeksema found that women tend to ruminate (think thoughts based on negative emotions and the events that led to these feelings) and men drink more alcohol to cope with bad feelings such as depression, anger and sadness.[6]

So what's the message? Stop dwelling on

the negativity of your situation. Yes, things may be dismal, but thinking about them over and over will not help you cope. It could lead you to depression.

Both men and women need to develop good ways to manage stress. Stress is a part of all of our lives. The goal is to manage it so it doesn't manage you.

TRAUMA OR CATASTROPHE

Catastrophes bring up feelings of helplessness and loss of control. If you've ever been through a tornado, flood or hurricane, you remember the feelings well. Or if you were diagnosed with an unforeseen illness or attacked by a rapist, you know the feelings of helplessness and loss of control.

Usually when a catastrophe hits, you have no previous experience to deal with the event. This creates stress and intense feelings of loss. Emotional and physical aftereffects are common. One common aftereffect is anxiety.

Dealing with catastrophe involves experiencing grief because of the loss. You go through stages of denial, shock, loneliness, guilt, anger, depression, bargaining. Most people bounce back and forth between these stages. Eventually you learn to accept the loss, or you become stuck in anxiety.

Your ability to recover from a calamity and not be immobilized by it depends, in part, on your resources. You need support, time and a strong belief in God. Grieving is a process.

Asking *why* doesn't help much when it comes to catastrophes. Usually the only answer we have is that we live in a fallen and sinful world. The Bible tells us troubles will come. God promises His presence no matter the circumstances of life.

It's easy to feel abandoned and unprotected by God. But you must have faith and believe the promises of God even when you don't *feel* they are true. Nothing happens away from His watchful eye. His promise is to bring something good out of ashes.

We can't understand His sovereignty. We don't have God's view of the big picture, so we must trust Him. It's OK to feel angry, depressed and shocked when calamity hits. Just don't get stuck there.

Allow the feelings to surface. Stress in the middle of calamity is normal. Call upon His name, and He will hear you. As you heal, the stress will lessen.

SINGLE-PARENTING STRESS

Single-parent families are more common today than intact nuclear families. A father, mother, grandparent, aunt, uncle or other family member can head these families.

No matter who parents, all single parents face similar stress. In order to better support single parents, sources of stress should be identified. Support is a buffer against stress and can be offered by other parents, friends, churches and family members.

So what are the unique challenges of being a single parent?

BREAKING FREE

MENTAL HEALTH FACT

Single Parenting and Stress

- *Single parents have no other parent to act as a buffer*—someone to take the kids for a few hours, share discipline or talk through a difficult situation. One women recently shared her frustration of trying to help her four-year-old daughter deal with a soccer coach. The child felt the coach was mean. After a long day of carting children to sports activities and not being able to attend the daughter's complete game, the mom didn't know if her child was overreacting because she missed her dad or whether the coach really was a problem. When married, the husband handled coaches. Exhausted from the day, unsure of what her daughter needed, she longed for someone to talk to about the coach or just take care of the situation. It was a small thing, but it felt big at the end of a full day.

- *Single parents are solely responsible for the household.* Some single parents carry the entire financial burden, others have to contend with partial or late alimony and child support payments, and still others deal with a lower standard of living because of dual child-rearing households. Single parents do it all—pay the bills, stay home for the cable guy, work on the car, help with homework, baths, whatever it takes to keep the household running. They are responsible for making sure everything works.

- *Single parents deal with ongoing custody and visitation issues.* The amount of stress in this area ranges from virtually none to severe, depending on how cooperative parents are about these issues post divorce.

- *Parental conflict can continue long after a divorce.* Couples are forced to work together for the good of their children. Some do a better job than others.

- *There is less time for single parents to spend with children* because of work and household demands.

- *Single parents have to deal with the aftermath of divorce* as it affects school performance and peer relationships.

- *Extended family relationships are disrupted* because of divorce, and single parents must figure out how and if these relationships will continue.

- *Single parents have to contend with dating and new relationships.* This can create problems if children are not ready to embrace new people into the family system.

~~~~~~~

This list only touches on some of the issues single parents regularly face. It is easy for a single parent to become overwhelmed because of all that is needed and expected. Single parents don't need pity or judgment. They can use your support. Pray for single parents, that God will give them the grace and strength to handle all that is before them. Then offer your support in a tangible way—give them a few hours break, be available to talk, carpool kids and do other helpful things. A little help goes a long way.

INFERTILITY

Over five million people of childbearing age in the United States are infertile, according to RESOLVE, the national infertility organization. Infertility is defined by the medical community as the inability to conceive after one year of unprotected sex, or the inability to carry pregnancy to live birth. It is usually considered a couple problem, even though one partner may carry the medical diagnosis.

Even though infertility is a health problem, the stress it places on couples can be enormous. Infertility is a disruption in the family life cycle and becomes a focal point of daily lives for affected couples. Coming to grips with the diagnosis often involves emotions associated with grief—shock, denial, anger, guilt, depression, weariness, isolation and ambivalence.

Infertility represents a negative life event that requires adjustment. Stress mounts as the problem remains unresolved. One of the most difficult aspects of infertility is the fact that the outcome is ambiguous. Because couples are uncertain as to whether or not pregnancy will be achieved, they are constantly dealing with loss or the threat of loss. So stressful is the experience that many couples request psychological services when they first contact an infertility clinic.

Infertility exhausts resources and affects multiple domains of a couple's life—marital and sexual relations, finances, employment, health and others. Couples find themselves mentally, physically and emotionally drained.

A mental health therapist trained in infertility issues can help couples cope with the physical and emotional stresses associated with infertility. Typically, therapists become involved when couples face difficult treatment decisions, have trouble communicating with one another or have different ideas about the direction of treatment. With help, it is possible to come through the crisis of infertility stronger than ever.

If you think you would benefit from talking to a therapist about the stresses of infertility, ask your doctor for a referral or contact your local mental health providers for the name of a trained therapist. Be aware that therapists bring to the therapy table a variety of values and ideas about reproductive procedures. It is important to find someone who will work within your value system and respect your decisions.

Balancing Work and Family

Charles was a midlevel manager working his way to an executive level position. The vice president of the company firmly believed Charles was a rising star in the company. All Charles needed to do was work hard and put in the long hours. There was only one problem. Charles's wife, Janet, resented his undying dedication to his job. At home with three small children, Janet wanted Charles to spend more time with the family. Tension between Janet and Charles was building. The couple needed help.

Charles and Janet represent many couples who struggle to find balance between the demands of work and home. Wives complain that husbands are more married to the office than to them. Men feel they are doing what they are supposed to do as men—provide for their families. The dilemma for many men is how to balance the needs of family life with career. Not attending to family needs has obvious consequences, but not attending to the job implies you aren't a serious contender for promotion.

Women who stay home sometimes envy the love affair men have with their work. Work can be exhilarating, exciting and even a frightening part of a man's life. Work often defines a man and plays into his feelings of self-worth. Career success means

Work should be challenging and fulfilling, but not the sole focus of being a man.

you are somebody. Men are taught that power, status and earning capacity are markers of masculinity. Value is measured by economic and occupational success.

Consequently, men have fears and anxieties about failure and measuring up. Are they good enough? Can they compete? Will they win? The pressure to perform can be intense and even be self-imposed.

At home, performance is rated through

relationship—a world of unclear rules and ever-changing demands. Women at home seem to have the edge when it comes to family rules and details about children and households. Control over outcome is not like work.

Men like Charles aren't up on the current issues at home. At times, Janet treats him like "a dummy," which makes the office more appealing. At work, Charles feels competent and in control.

Men like Charles need balance, but they don't always know how to achieve it. Balance is a biblical concept dating back to the Garden of Eden. Man worked and then rested. Work should be challenging and fulfilling, but not the sole focus of being a man.

B R E A K I N G F R E E
M E N T A L H E A L T H F A C T

Balancing Work and Family

If you are a man out of balance with work and family, try these steps:

- Learn to set limits on the job.

- Address fears of failure or not

measuring up to preconceived standards or unrealistic expectations.

- Check out what the Bible has to say about your worth apart from what you do for a living.

- Define yourself through your relationship with God. He gives unconditional love and approval of who you are.

- Pray for wisdom and sensitivity to balance the needs of family and career.

- Reevaluate your current position. Is what you do worth the sacrifice made in other areas of your life? If not, ask God to direct you to a new opportunity or negotiate more balance.

~~~~~~~~~~

AGING

Seniors can be innovators. That's the opinion of many, including Maggie Kuhn, a cofounder of the Grey Panthers. Aging is not a time to shrivel up and die. It's a time to use gained wisdom and experience to form new ideas for the future and upcoming generations. Take pride in your age, history and life experiences. The interplay of your wisdom and experience with the energy and freshness of younger generations is needed.

CARE-GIVING

You are a forty-six-year-old woman, married, employed and living near your seventy-seven-year-old mother. According to a 1997 survey given by the National Alliance for Caregiving, you are the typical caregiver for an older person. You join approximately 12 million other adult children in this task. Of the 12 million, three quarters of them are daughters.[7]

Even though you choose to give care, it can create an emotional strain. The National Family Caregivers Association reports that almost half of all caregivers suffer from depression; two-thirds regularly feel frustrated; and two of five feel "debilitated" due to the changes in family dynamics.[8]

Ever since the term "sandwich generation" was born, self-help groups, facts and information abound on how to make and execute various practical tasks involved in care-taking parents. But it is the emotional part of care-giving that trips us up.

The Adult Caretaker

What are some of the emotional issues involved for the adult caretaker?

- *Your own mortality.* Care-taking an aging parent causes you to think about your own aging process and eventual death.

- *Who will take care of you if you need help?* You may begin to think hard about your own options and plans for care.

- *Unresolved parent-child problems.* The hope of many is that taking care of a parent may reverse a damaged relationship. When this doesn't happen, it can be even more distressing for the adult child. For example, a daughter might find the father who never gave approval still not giving his approval, or the mother who was depressed and emotionally unavailable still emotionally distant.

- *Remorse about the past.* You may have regrets that were never discussed.

- *Reversal of roles.* You become the parent, and the parent becomes the child. This reversal of roles requires adjustment for both child and parent.

None of the above issues are handled easily. You may need to spend time in prayer and ask God to give you patience, understanding and resources to confront the issues you face. Go to Him.

Honor your parents no matter how difficult the care-taking becomes. Remember their dignity. They desire to be independent and self-sufficient as long as possible. Aging parents often worry that they are a burden to their adult children. They are not used to their children having to do for them.

Be aware of the emotional issues raised, and then work on managing them. If you need the help of a therapist, find one who will counsel you from a Christian perspective and who specializes in treatment with the aged. Take advantage of help and support so you don't become one of the seriously stressed.

BREAKING FREE
PRAYER FOR YOU

Lord, I don't know why I am in this position. I just know the stress is difficult, and sometimes it seems I can't go on. But You can help me and give me hope. As I think about the specifics of my life, help me practice new ways to cope and, most importantly, learn to trust You in all things.

CHAPTER 6

BREAKING FREE SUMMARY

I am not afraid of storms, for I am learning how to sail my ship.

—LOUISA MAY ALCOTT

Let's review the steps to break free from stress.

1. *Stop and think about the kinds and type of stress in your life* (chapter one). Remember stress can be positive and negative; it can come from an event, a transition, the environment, development, your perception and/or personality type.

2. *Identify personal stress* (chapter two). Take the stress test. Fill out the Current Stress Chart and note how many stressors are currently affecting you. Are they pre-

dictable or unpredictable, major
or minor, acute or chronic?

3. *Use your number one resource—*
   God (chapter three). Align your
   behavior, and conform to His
   image. Renew your mind. Stand in
   faith. Confess His promises. Jesus
   asks you to cast your cares on
   Him. Don't act in your own
   power, but depend on God. Use
   the biblical prescription for worry
   found in Philippians 4.

4. *Use the break-free strategies for*
   physical and mental release of
   stress (chapter four).

5. *Apply these strategies to common*
   sources of stress (chapter five).

B R E A K I N G ☙ F R E E
M E N T A L   H E A L T H F A C T

Break-Free Strategies for Stress

Physical

- Deep muscle relaxation
- Deep breathing and relaxation
- Support
- Regulate sleep

- Make environmental changes
- Improve your diet and exercise
- Give up smoking
- Cut out unnecessary activities
- Make small changes

Mental and Cognitive

- Prayer and meditation
- Be assertive
- Learn to say no
- Develop humor
- Problem-solve

THE HOPE

When stress seems overwhelming, revisit the story of Joseph found in Genesis. He was his father Jacob's favorite son, yet Joseph's world became a living nightmare. Sold into slavery by his envious brothers, dragged to Egypt to serve Potiphar (an officer of Pharaoh), amazingly Joseph prospers. Then, just when life seemed to be taking a positive turn, Potiphar's wife, spurned by Joseph, accuses him of attempted rape. In an act of mercy, he is given prison, not death. Yet, he spends years serving a sentence he doesn't deserve. Finally, he is summoned to interpret two dreams for Pharaoh, and God reveals their meaning to Joseph. As a reward, Pharaoh elevates him to prime minister with a port-folio to prepare Egypt for seven years of famine. Joseph's new position of power brings him back in contact with the very brothers who had betrayed him. In a complete reversal, Joseph now has the power to decide the fate of family members who betrayed him.

What is remarkable about Joseph is his response to stress. He is faced with unpredictability and unfairness—thrown in a pit, sold into slavery, scorned by a woman, jailed for a crime he didn't commit. All of these stressors are major and chronic, putting Joseph at risk for serious physical illness and mental breakdown.

What you notice as you read through the account of his life is this: "But the LORD was with Joseph and showed him mercy…" (Gen. 39:21). When he revealed himself to his family, a time that could have turned ugly, he shows incredible understanding of the sovereignty of God: "So now it was not you who sent me here, but God" (Gen. 45:8, NKJV). "But as for you, you meant evil against me; but God meant it for good, in order to bring it about as it is this day, to save many people alive" (Gen. 50:20, NKJV).

Joseph overcame incredible difficulty. Under stress he didn't give in, give up or blame God. He knew God promised to take care of him.

It is possible to respond to stress like Joseph if you believe that God is with you, that He shows you mercy and that He will deliver you. God's ways are not always our ways because He sees the big picture. Release your burdens to Him. Believe that He is actively involved in your life and that He is always present, ready to help. Depend on God to get you through times of stress, and you won't be disappointed.

BREAKING FREE

PRAYER FOR YOU

Lord, help me to persevere through difficulty, never forgetting Your hand is on my life. I don't always understand why things happen, but I do trust You to direct my paths and walk through any valley with me. You are my comfort and source of peace. Thank You. Amen.

NOTES

CHAPTER 1

1. *Psychology at Work: How does stress affects us?* Adapted from *The Stress Solution* by Lyle H. Miller, Ph.D. and Alma Dell Smith, Ph.D. Retrieved 5-8-02 from http://helping.apa.org/work/stress 2.html. Copyright © 1997 American Psychological Association.
2. *Stress*, WebMD Health. Definition retrieved 5-8-02 from http://my.webmd.com/content/article/1680.51976.
3. *What are the biological mechanics of acute stress?* Reviewed by Dr. Charlotte Grayson for WebMD. Retrieved 5-8-02 from http//my.webmd.com/content/article/1680.52658.

CHAPTER 2

1. T. H. Holmes and R. H. Rahe, "The social readjustment rating scale," *Journal of Psychosomatic Research* 2 (1967): 213–218.
2. Ibid., reprinted with permission of Elsevier Science Publications. Used by permission.

CHAPTER 5

1. Patrick A. McGuire, "Worker stress, health reaching critical point," *APA*

Monitor Online, vol. 30, no. 5 (May 1999): www.apa.org/monitor/may99/mosn.html. Retrieved online May 15, 2000.

2. "Mom's stress may affect early child development," *APA Monitor Online*, vol. 30, no. 9 (October 1999): www.apa.org/monitor/oct99/c14.html. Retrieved online May 15, 2000.

3. Joel Schwarz, "Good news for expectant couples: Arrival of first baby doesn't mean wife's marital satisfaction has to take big nose dive," *University of Washington News and Events* (October 24, 2000): www.washington.edu/newsroom/news/2000archive/10-00archive/K103400a.html. Retrieved online July 8, 2002.

4. Ibid.

5. Ibid.

6. "Men and women handle negative situations differently, study suggests," *APA Monitor Online*, vol. 30, no. 9 (October 1999): www.apa.org/monitor/oct99/nb61.html. Retrieved online May 15, 2000.

7. Testimony for a joint hearing of the United States Senate, Special Committee on the Aging, and the Health, Education, Labor and Pension

Subcommittee on Aging, February 6, 2002, by Gail Gibson Hunt, executive director, National Alliance for Caregiving. Retrieved from www.senate. gov/~labor/hearings-2002/feb2002/ 020602wit/hunt.pdf.
8. Ibid.

Your Walk With God Can Be Even Deeper...

With *Charisma* magazine, you'll be informed and inspired by the features and stories about what the Holy Spirit is doing in the lives of believers today.

Each issue:
- Brings you exclusive world-wide reports to rejoice over.
- Keeps you informed on the latest news from a Christian perspective.
- Includes miracle-filled testimonies to build your faith.
- Gives you access to relevant teaching and exhortation from the most respected Christian leaders of our day.

Call 1-800-829-3346 for 3 FREE trial issues
Offer #A2CCHB

If you like what you see, then pay the invoice of $22.97 (**saving over 51% off the cover price**) and receive 9 more issues (12 in all). Otherwise, write "cancel" on the invoice, return it, and owe nothing.

Experience the Power of Spirit-Led Living

Charisma Offer #A2CCHB
P.O. Box 420234
Palm Coast, Florida 32142-0234
www.charismamag.com

2577